C o n t e n t s

ABBREVIATIONS

GAO   General Accounting Office

ADP   automatic data processing

SRI   Stanford Research Institute

CHAPTER 1

INTRODUCTION

In recent years, a new type of criminal has appeared--the computer criminal. Well-publicized crimes have demonstrated that computer-based systems are vulnerable to criminal activity, and hundreds of computer-related crimes have been detected. The dollar value of reported computer-related bank embezzlements, for example, ranged from about $1,000 to almost $7 million. 1/

Faced with the possibility of such activity in Government, we reviewed computer-related crimes in Government organizations. Since we promulgate Federal accounting and auditing standards and work with other levels of government to help improve their standards and procedures, our objectives in this review were to:

--Determine whether computer-related crimes are occurring in Government.

--Relate methods used by computer criminals to weaknesses in controls in the systems in which they committed the crimes.

--Examine the internal audit procedures used to review the operations affected by the crimes to determine whether changes in audit procedures, standards, or guidelines are needed.

--Identify ways to help prevent and detect future crimes.

WHAT IS A COMPUTER-RELATED CRIME?

We define computer-related crimes as acts of intentionally caused losses to the Government or personal gains to individuals related to the design, use, or operation of the systems in which they are committed. Computer-based data processing systems are comprised of more than the computer hardware and the programs (software) that run on them. The systems include the organizations and procedures--some manual--for preparing input to the computer and using output from it. Computer-related crimes may result from preparing false input to systems and misuse of output as well as more technically sophisticated crimes, such as altering computer programs.

1/Donn B. Parker, Susan Nycum, S. Stephen Oura., Computer Abuse, Stanford Research Institute, 1973 (NTIS Pub. No. PB231-320/AS).

1

We have used the terms "crimes" and "criminals" throughout this report in lay sense. Many of the examples reported have resulted in criminal convictions. However, for various reasons, some of the incidents did not result in criminal proceedings.

FEDERAL MANAGERS HAVE RESPONSIBILITY TO ESTABLISH EFFECTIVE CONTROLS

Under the Budget and Accounting Procedures Act of 1950, the head of each Government agency is required to establish and maintain systems of internal control to safeguard assets. The same legislation requires us to prescribe accounting standards, to work with agencies in developing systems, and to audit agencies to determine the adequacy of internal controls over financial operations. In addition, we are responsible for approving agencies' accounting systems when they conform to standards prescribed by the Comptroller General.

In conjunction with the Secretary of the Treasury and the Office of Management and Budget, we have developed accounting principles and standards to be observed by executive agencies. These were published in the Comptroller General's Manual for Guidance of Federal Agencies.

Section 7 of title 2 of the manual states that an accounting system is an integral part of management control and should help safeguard "all funds, property, and other resources for which the agency is responsible * * *" from "* * * misuse [and] misappropriation * * *."

Internal auditing is one of the essential tools of management, complementing other elements of management control. Using automatic data processing (ADP) as the basis for a system requires increased emphasis on review of internal controls, because computer-based systems centralize and concentrate data processing steps.

HOW INFORMATION ON CRIMES WAS GATHERED

We obtained information on 69 cases of improper use of computers from various investigative offices. These cases, which are listed in appendix I, totaled over $2 million. They do not represent all the computer crimes involving the Federal Government since agencies do not customarily differentiate between computer-related and other crimes. Moreover, there may be a large number of crimes which have not yet been detected or reported. For example, in just one inventory system, military investigative officials estimated that only a fifth of all losses were reported and that 80 percent of all thefts may have been computer related. Our study was aimed only at those crimes already reported.

We reviewed in detail 12 of the cases representing a cross section of the types of crimes reported to date. The details of our method of examination are in chapter 7.

CHAPTER 2

THE NATURE OF GOVERNMENT COMPUTER CRIMES

A wide variety of computer-related crimes in all levels
of Government has been discovered. Most have been committed
by persons who possess only limited technical knowledge of
computers; that is, users of ADP systems rather than persons
with more technical knowledge such as programers, operators,
or analysts. Of the 69 cases in our files, at least 50 were
committed by system users, not ADP personnel.

A Stanford Research Institute (SRI) report prepared
for us notes that, although sophisticated computer crimes
are the ones that get publicity, most criminals discovered so
far used unsophisticated methods. Moreover, most committed
their crimes within their own work environments.

Our review of Government cases shows results similar to
those in the Stanford Research report.

WHAT KINDS OF CRIMES ARE OCCURRING?

We can best illustrate the varied types of crimes by
giving some examples of cases gathered from agency records.

The majority of cases--about 62 percent--involved persons
preparing fraudulent input to computer-based systems. (See
chart on p. 6.) Several variations of this method have been
discovered.

Supply systems are particularly vulnerable to fraudulent
input. In one case, a perpetrator used a computer terminal
to ascertain the location and availability of items desired by
outside conspirators. Once he located those items, the perpetrator caused the system to prepare fraudulent requisitioning
documents. Then he used the documents to obtain the items
he wanted, took the items from the installation, and sold
them to the outside parties. Although the total amount of
property stolen through computerized supply systems cannot
easily be determined, the value of one such theft in our
case files was about $53,000. Another loss of over $300,000
was averted when discrepancies were discovered accidentally
and the material recovered.

Many cases discovered to date in which the individuals
involved prepared fraudulent input involve systems that make
direct payments to individuals or businesses. These include
fraudulent payroll, social welfare, and compensation transactions as well as payments for nonexistent goods and services. For example:

--A Government employee who had helped automate an accounting system introduced fraudulent payment vouchers into the system. The computer could not recognize that the transactions were fraudulent and issued checks payable to fictitious companies set up by the employee and his accomplices. These checks were sent directly to banks where the conspirators had opened accounts for the companies. The criminals then withdrew the funds from the accounts. Officials estimated the Government may have paid this employee and his accomplices $100,000 for goods that had never been delivered.

--A supervisory clerk responsible for entering claim transactions to a computer-based social welfare system found she could introduce fictitious claims on behalf of accomplices and they would receive the benefits. She was able to process over $90,000 in claims (authorities believe it might have been up to $250,000) before she was discovered through an anonymous telephone tip.

Another type of act, which has occurred in several agencies, is the unauthorized use of computers by ADP personnel. An engineer who was no longer employed at a computer installation managed to continue using the equipment for his own purposes. Before he was discovered, he had used over $4,000 worth of computer time. At another installation, a programer used a self-initiated training program to obtain use of his agency's computer system. But instead of working on the training exercise, he was developing his own computer programs which he hoped to sell.

Computer-related crime does not always lead to direct monetary losses. The manager of a non-Federal computer center processing personal information was able to steal some of this data and sell it to outside parties who were not authorized to use it. Although the Government did not lose any money, the privacy of individuals whose data records were involved was violated, and this is of concern in protecting the privacy of personal information.

For convenience, we have categorized the methods used to commit known Government computer crimes.

Category 1--initiation of fraudulent records (input)

Includes such crimes as deliberately falsifying input documents or records, entering counterbalancing transactions, and falsifying claims by reuse of supporting documents previously processed.

TYPES OF COMPUTER-RELATED CRIMES
IN GOVERNMENT

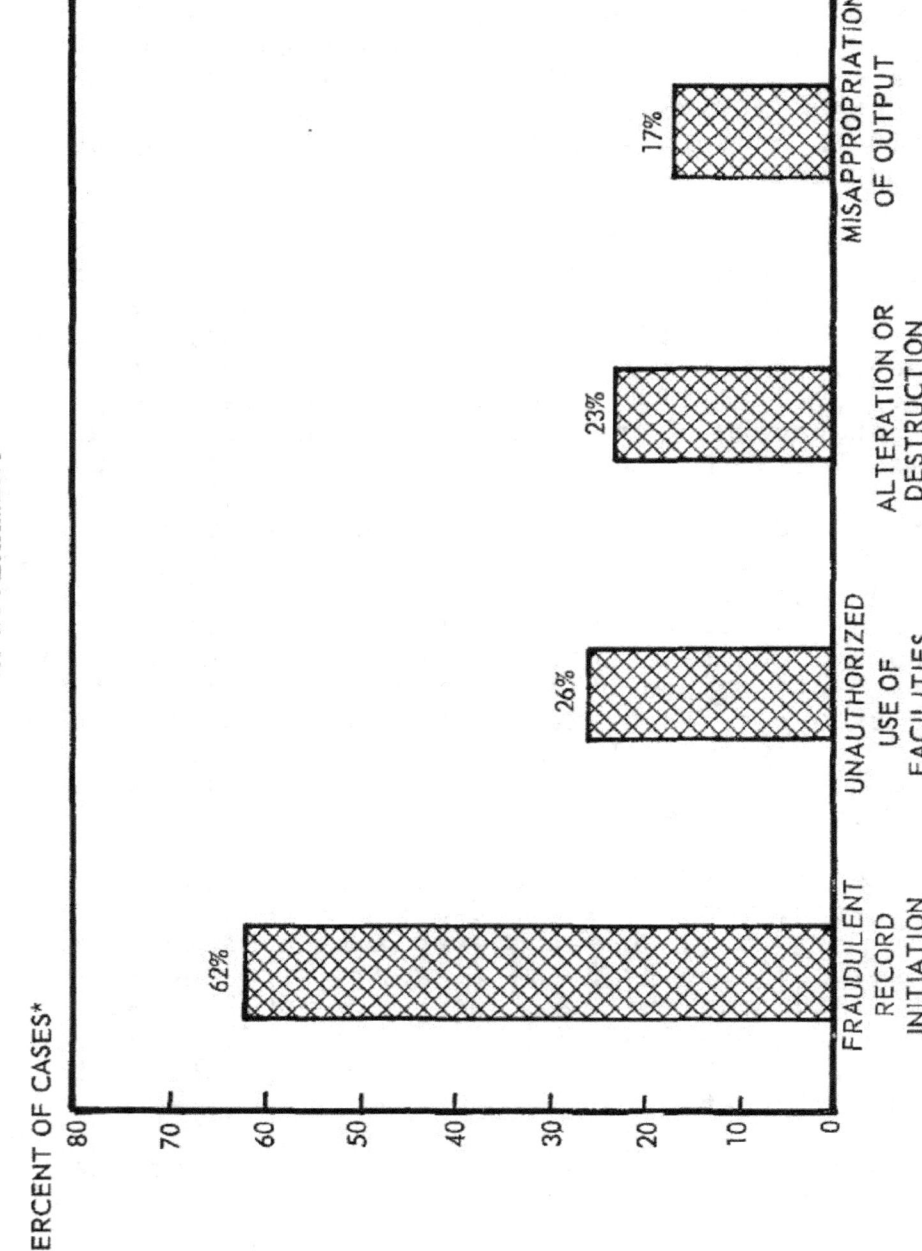

PERCENT OF CASES*

*PERCENTS TOTAL MORE THAN 100% BECAUSE SOME CASES APPLY TO MORE THAN ONE CATEGORY.

6

Category 2--unauthorized or inappropriate
use of facilities and supplies

Includes developing salable programs on organizations'
computers, doing commercial service-bureau-type work for
outsiders on organizations' computers, using remote terminals
for personal benefit, and duplicating magnetic files and
selling them.

Category 3--processing alteration
or destruction

Includes such crimes as sabotage or altering information
recorded in the files affecting pay, promotion, or assignment
and bypassing existing controls to enter unauthorized changes.
These crimes could be done by operators intervening to per-
form unauthorized processing, resulting in gain to the opera-
tor or his accomplice, or by programers altering computer
programs.

Category 4--misappropriation of output

Includes such crimes as misappropriating returned
checks and eliminating or altering notices designed to
provide controls and balances.

The chart on page 6 shows the percentage of cases in
our files which relate to each of the categories.

HOW DO GOVERNMENT CRIMES COMPARE TO
THOSE IN THE PRIVATE SECTOR?

The Stanford Research Institute report indicates the
same types of crimes occur in both the public and private
sectors. However, the cases we reviewed involve a greater
proportion of financial frauds than those in the SRI files
(67 percent versus 33 percent) and a smaller proportion of
vandalism and unauthorized use of services (3 percent Government versus 40 percent SRI). In both sets of files, the
majority of crimes were committed by systems users, but the
proportion of user crimes is larger in Government.

The size of the average loss in private sector crimes
is higher than in our Government cases. According to another
SRI report, the average loss for each case in 144 cases since
1963 was $450,000. The average loss of the Government cases,
for which a dollar loss was applicable and was determined,
was about $44,000. (See app. I.)

We do not know why the average losses in detected
Government cases are smaller than those in the private sector.

7

But, from a security standpoint, Government systems are similar to those in private businesses. Therefore, as the SRI report to us points out, there should be equal opportunity and temptation for the perpetration of computer crimes.

WHY DO THESE CRIMES OCCUR?

In every case we reviewed in detail, the incidents were directly traceable to weaknesses in system controls. These weaknesses were the result of deficient systems designs, improper implementation of controls by operating personnel, or a combination of both. Moreover, the weaknesses were in basic management controls, such as separation of duties and physical access control over facilities.

The primary reason weaknesses in system controls existed was that management failed to recognize the importance of controlling systems. This lack of emphasis affected both the way systems were designed and the extent to which operating personnel enforced controls.

Managers can use internal auditors as an important part of management control. But agencies' internal audit groups vary greatly in how they review ADP systems. Often the auditors were not aware of crimes that demonstrated weaknesses in internal control systems.

The following chapters explain the types of control weaknesses which have been exploited, the importance of management emphasis on controlling systems, and the roles played by auditors in the cases we reviewed.

CHAPTER 3

CRIMINALS EXPLOITED WEAKNESSES IN

BASIC MANAGEMENT CONTROLS

System controls are designed to protect the assets of an organization. Thus, it is not surprising that, in committing their crimes, perpetrators take advantage of system control weaknesses. What may be surprising is that the weaknesses exploited are mostly basic management controls long recognized as being necessary to insure proper operations.

The characteristics of a satisfactory system of internal controls include:

1. An organizational plan that segregates duties of individuals to minimize their opportunity for misuse or misappropriation of the entity's resources.

2. A system of authorization and record procedures adequate to provide effective accounting control over assets, liabilities, revenues, and expenses.

3. An established system of practices to be followed for each duty and function of the organizational departments.

4. An effective system of internal review.

The most common weaknesses which have been exploited in our cases were in (1) separation of duties and (2) physical control over facilities and supplies. Sometimes these weaknesses are due to poorly designed systems, but in 7 of the 12 cases we reviewed in detail, controls or procedures existed but were not enforced by operating personnel.

INADEQUATE SEPARATION OF DUTIES AND POOR PHYSICAL CONTROLS ARE THE MOST COMMON WEAKNESSES

Using computers compresses activities into fewer hands. Under such circumstances, management should critically evaluate the amount of control any one individual exercises over processing steps. In 7 of the 12 cases, inadequate separation of duties was a major weakness contributing to the perpetrators' successes.

In one social benefit program, the perpetrator was a system user, a representative responsible for certifying the eligibility of benefit recipients. But he also prepared data to be put into the ADP system for controlling and issuing negotiable coupons. Although the system identified some discrepancies, no one investigated or reconciled the discrepancies. Using his position in the organization to his own advantage, he processed a series of fraudulent claims, causing coupons be be sent to accomplices not eligible to receive them. The coupons were then redeemed by accomplices. No one reviewed the validity of transactions initiated by this clerk, and he did not even have to prepare backup source documents to support the fraudulent claims.

ADP personnel also can take advantage of too much concentrated authority and responsibility. One of our cases involved the manager of a small non-Federal computer center. This person had authority to establish procedures at the center, revise those procedures at his own discretion, and circumvent established operational controls with little or no review by supervisors or system users. He used his position to sell information on private citizens to special interest groups which paid him an estimated $48,000 for that information. As previously stated, this violated the privacy of persons whose records he sold.

Another common weakness is poor physical control of facilities and supplies. Some examples of these weaknesses include unauthorized access to computer rooms, unauthorized use of terminals, unrestricted access to computer tape files, and free access to documents authorizing transactions. Such weaknesses led directly to improprieties in 5 of the 12 cases.

ONCE DESIGNED, CONTROLS MUST BE USED

Even though a system design may include adequate controls, they are ineffective unless persons using and operating the systems are required to use the controls.

One Federal installation followed a common practice prohibiting programers from operating computer equipment except in special circumstances and only with approval from the appropriate division chief. However, authorized computer operators allowed programers to operate equipment on several occasions without knowing whether the programers had proper approval to do so. Operators said they did this to help programers' test their programs, and the operators even started the equipment for them. Unfortunately, one of the programers was using the computer to develop his own programs, which he hoped to sell commercially.

The SRI report states the most effective safeguards against most computer-related crimes discovered to date in the private sector are separation of duties and other management controls that are traditionally included in any well-designed system.

Failings in these same areas--in basic management controls--contribute to Government crimes, too. Although computer technology requires that these controls be implemented using more sophisticated techniques, they are still essential. Management should be concerned first with basic administrative controls to tighten system security.

CHAPTER 4

MANAGEMENT DOES NOT PLACE SUFFICIENT EMPHASIS

ON CONTROLLING SYSTEMS

Primary responsibility for control of operations rests with top management--a legal requirement in Federal agencies as well as a tenet of sound management practice. Our review showed that managers often do not place sufficient emphasis on controlling systems, and this lack of emphasis results in poorly designed or inadequately enforced controls. This presents increased opportunities to criminals.

MANAGEMENT PLACED PRIORITY ON MAKING SYSTEMS OPERATIONAL RATHER THAN ON CONTROLLING THEM

Managers of organizations involved in many of the 12 cases we reviewed had primarily emphasized making their systems operational; control was not emphasized.

In one case involving a social compensation system, automatic data processing personnel told us their organization's processing was built around second-generation computers and had no fraud-oriented controls built in. When they converted to more modern equipment, the system was not redesigned because of pressure to get the new computers running. An employee submitted fraudulent claims to this system, and the system sent her checks totaling over $15,000.

Another case involved a contractor ordering Government-furnished material for approved contracts directly through a Government supply system, using a remote terminal device. No controls existed to insure that the material ordered (by type or quantity) was appropriate to a given contract, and the contractor requisitioned over $300,000 worth of material to which it was not entitled and for which it would not have paid. In designing the system, officials had emphasized speeding up the requisition process; they considered time more critical than controls that might delay delivery.

Management should give attention to controlling systems as well as to implementing them. Managers should continuously assess operations to insure a proper balance between performance of systems and control over assets.

MANAGEMENT DID NOT ASSESS POTENTIAL
THREATS TO SYSTEMS

The National Bureau of Standards published in June 1974 Federal Information Processing Standards Publication 31, entitled "Guidelines for Automatic Data Processing Physical Security and Risk Management." This publication provides suggestions for managers in assessing potential threats and losses to systems in terms of both physical and data security.

A similar risk assessment concept is proposed in Federal Information Processing Standards Publication 41, "Computer Security Guidelines for Implementing the Privacy Act of 1974." This publication states the premise that the first step in improving a system's security is to analyze its security risks.

Although the importance of such analyses is now gaining recognition, most of the organizations involved in the cases we reviewed had not made such an analysis before being victimized. One agency did make a threat study after investigating a crime and, as a result, implemented several new controls.

Other agencies now are starting to analyze threats to computer systems. One example is the U.S. Army Intelligence Agency, which uses a threat model to evaluate security at ADP installations. This model describes the ADP installation being reviewed and is used by the agency's staff to ascertain potential security problems at the installation. Analyses of potential threats and losses to identify the need for and types of cost-effective controls are necessary for managers to carry out their responsibilities to control assets.

The Stanford Research Institute report points out that one of the key elements in operational security is management support. Inadequate control often can be traced to lack of management attention to the problem. In view of the crimes discovered to date and the potential for more losses, it is important that top managers recognize the need for proper security, systems controls, and supervision.

CHAPTER 5

IMPROVEMENT NEEDED IN AUDITS OF SYSTEM CONTROLS

Internal auditing is an important part of the management control function. It complements other elements of management control, and it provides independent judgment on the ways managers have carried out their responsibilities.

Our Standards for Audit of Governmental Organizations, Programs, Activities, and Functions require evaluations of systems of internal control.

Proper auditing of system controls and procedures can detect weaknesses that facilitate criminal activity and can help discourage potential criminals. But Federal agencies' internal audit groups vary greatly in how they review automatic data processing systems. In 9 of the 12 cases we studied, auditors had not reviewed controls in the systems involved. To plan their work properly, audit staffs should be made aware of criminal activity which resulted from weaknesses in controls. But often they are not.

PROPER AUDITS CAN DETECT WEAKNESSES
THAT LEAD TO CRIMES

The auditor's responsibility in detecting fraud is the subject of current controversy. However, adequate reviews of internal controls can and do help detect weaknesses that facilitate crimes, thus helping management prevent them. Audits or special reviews in 13 of the 69 cases in our files-- about 19 percent--actually did result in the discovery of improprieties.

Auditors reviewing system controls in two of the cases identified and reported weaknesses in them. In both cases, the auditors made recommendations to correct the weaknesses, but in each case management action was inadequate. The weaknesses continued to exist, and the criminals took advantage of them.

The Stanford Research Institute report points out that auditing can be a deterrent to potential criminals. Computer criminals are typically not "professional" criminals, but persons who have encountered difficulties on a short-term basis and who commit their crimes to help them solve their problems. They experience great personal suffering when their acts are discovered. Therefore, a highly visible and active audit function could dissuade them from attempting crimes.

14

AUDITS OF CONTROLS HAD NOT BEEN MADE

We found wide variations in the approaches Federal agencies' internal audit staffs have taken to review ADP systems. Some auditors become involved during system development, and some do not. Use of specific audit techniques, such as test decks, retrieval packages, and specially written computer audit programs, varies widely. Most agencies believe their audit staffs should have knowledge about various aspects of ADP--such as design, operation, and controls--but the auditors' own estimates of their abilities to address these areas show great differences.

No internal audits of system controls had been made in 5 of the 12 cases. In four other cases, investigative officials, not auditors, had reviewed specific systems controls as they related to crimes already detected. Even the one agency in which auditors' reviews had revealed system weaknesses, Federal officials responsible for the the audits stated that the programs involved were so large the agency did not have the resources to make onsite inspections or followup reviews on recommendations. They stated they had to do much of their work through correspondence and meetings. They did not assure themselves management had taken appropriate action on reported deficiencies.

Although we cannot say that audits of controls would have detected or prevented all 69 incidents, such audits are recognized as an important part of good overall management control. Some agency officials told us of specific plans to review systems procedures and controls, and some had been reviewing them regularly. Others had not, and overall we found audits of controls either inadequate or ineffective.

AUDITORS SHOULD BE INFORMED OF CRIMINAL ACTIVITY INDICATING CONTROL WEAKNESSES

Information on frauds and unusual irregularities should be made available to us and to others in the agencies who may legitimately inquire into them. This is pointed out in title 7 of our Manual for Guidance of Federal Agencies. But agency internal auditors often had not been informed about computer-related crimes so they could consider their effect on audit procedures. In several of the cases we reviewed, auditors told us our inquiry was the first time they had heard of the crimes.

Some agencies' audit officials told us they did have informal cooperative procedures with investigators in their agencies. One agency, which now recognizes the need to share information, told us it is establishing formal cooperative procedures at policy levels as well as at working levels.

For internal auditors to be responsive to needs of management and the organization, they should have information necessary to develop adequate work procedures. Sharing information on criminal activity involving systems problems at various organizational levels is necessary to insure good planning of audits.

CHAPTER 5

CONCLUSIONS AND RECOMMENDATIONS

The number of computer-related crimes in Government as well as in the private sector is cause for concern about how well systems are being controlled. The dollar values of Government cases we know about are not as large as those in some crimes in private businesses, but we cannot be sure whether factors in Government systems prevent larger losses or whether we simply have not uncovered larger crimes.

It is clear the potential for computer-related crimes exists, especially since reliance on the computer is increasing. We know that weaknesses in the design and the execution of controls in automatic data processing systems make it easier to commit crimes. We have evidence that security surrounding Federal computer installations and applications is about the same as that in the private sector, and in our own reviews of Federal agencies' systems, we continue to find weaknesses in design and enforcement of controls.

Computers have added a new dimension to the potential for crimes. They can make crimes harder to detect because computer-based systems usually provide fewer written records of transactions. These systems naturally concentrate processing in fewer hands and make proper separation of duties more difficult to achieve. The concentration of asset information in easily changed form increases the potential size of each loss.

As a result of these characteristics, there should be a more systematic approach to preventing and detecting crimes in computer-based systems than was necessary for manual systems. This means better internal control and more effort to see that the system is operating as designed.

RECOMMENDATIONS

Although Government-wide standards on internal controls and on audits of internal controls have existed for several years, heads of Federal organizations need to insure that adequate controls are designed into computer-based systems serving them and that those controls are functioning properly.

We recommend that the heads of the organizations which gave us information on computer-related crimes which have

occurred in their departments or agencies--the Departments
of Defense (Army, Navy, and Air Force); Agriculture; the
Treasury; Health, Education, and Welfare; the Interior;
and the Veterans Administration--take steps to insure
that systems in their organizations and in those supporting
programs they fund have:

--An organizational plan that segregates the duties
of individuals to minimize their opportunity for misuse or misappropriation of the entity's resources.

--A system of authorization and record procedures
adequate to provide effective accounting control
over assets, liabilities, revenues, and expenses.

--An established system of practices to be followed
for each duty and function of the organizational
element.

--An effective system of internal review. This
includes an internal audit staff that has train-
ing adequate to review and evaluate computer-
based system controls and that does such
reviews both when systems are being designed and
after they have become operational.

If crimes occur, they should be analyzed to
pinpoint the internal control weaknesses that may have
facilitated them. Therefore, we also recommend that
analyses of such crimes be made and results provided to
managers, designers, investigators, and auditors to help
them strengthen their operations and procedures.

Although we are making the above recommendations to
those organizations which gave us information on cases they
discovered, all departments and agencies that use computers
or sponsor programs in which computers are used are equally
vulnerable to computer-related crimes. We are therefore
sending copies of this report to other departments and
agencies for their information and use; we urge them to
take the steps stated above to insure the propriety of
their operations.

We believe the guidance on internal controls, internal
audit, and accounting methods provided in our Policy and
Procedures Manual for the Guidance of Federal Agencies
and in our audit standards, gives appropriate general
criteria. In determining whether an agency's accounting
system meets the standards for approval by the Comptroller
General, we always review the internal controls designed

into the system to be sure that they are sufficient.
A special check is made of computer controls whenever
a computer is involved.

In addition to the above matters, we are developing
some more detailed guidance which we plan to distribute
to departments and agencies in the near future. These
will include:

--Information on various Federal internal audit
  groups' work in ADP systems reviews, highlighting
  procedures and techniques which may be useful
  to others.

--Audit guides for evaluating automated systems.

--Audit guides for assessing the reliability of
  computer-produced information.

--Our criteria for evaluating automated accounting
  systems' designs for approval.

We are providing copies of this report to all Federal
departments and agencies to help them take appropriate steps
to achieve the necessary internal control over their
computer systems.

AGENCY COMMENTS

We gave departments and agencies that provided us information on computer-related crimes an opportunity to comment on our report. Each of them that did comment agreed
with our conclusions and recommendations.

CHAPTER 7

SCOPE OF REVIEW

We initially requested information on discovered cases of computer-related crimes from the investigative agencies listed below. These agencies generally did not classify case files as computer related, so their responses were based on file searches and, in some instances, on personal recollections of agents or attorneys.

Using this method, we obtained background information on 74 cases. Our examination showed that 69 of these cases fit our definition of computer-related crimes. (See p. 1.)

Agencies which gave us information on cases were:

1. Department of the Army, Criminal Investigations Division Command.

2. Department of the Navy, Navy Investigative Service.

3. Department of the Air Force, Office of Special Investigations.

4. Department of Justice:

    a. Executive Office for United States Attorneys.
    b. Federal Bureau of Investigation.

5. Department of Agriculture, Office of Investigation.

6. Department of the Treasury, Internal Revenue Service.

7. Department of Health, Education, and Welfare, Social Security Administration.

8. Department of the Interior, Division of Investigation.

9. Veterans Administration, Investigation and Security Services.

We selected 12 representative cases to review in detail, sending staff to the sites where the incidents occurred. The cases selected included four direct payment system cases, one personnel system case, five supply system cases, and one case in which personal information derived from Federal sources was used by a non-Federal agency. In three of these cases, we were able to interview the perpetrators of the crimes.

Our work at the sites included interviews with both ADP and functional users who had knowledge of the perpetrators and of their duties. In addition, we interviewed investigative staffs at the local sites to obtain additional information on the incidents. We interviewed local audit staffs and headquarters officials to learn what audit procedures had been used in covering the operations of systems involved.

Mr. Donn B. Parker of the Stanford Research Institute, who has been studying computer abuse since 1966, prepared a report for us based on his information. His files contain over 380 cases.

CASES

INCLUDED IN OUR REVIEW

Description/ amount of loss	Method used by perpetrator			
	Fraudulent record initiation	Improper use of facilities	Processing alteration	Misappropriation of output
Fraudulent direct payments:				
1. $ 3,680	X			
2. 250,000	X			
3. 1,120	X			
4. 28,000	X			
5. 100,000	X			
6. 25,000	X			
7. (a)	X			
8. 8,000	X		X	
9. 14,000	X			X
10. 15,480	X			X
11. 79,780	X			
12. 30,000	X			
13. 134,000	X			
14. (a)	X			
15. 16,113	X			
16. (a)	X			
17. 371	X			
18. 4,400	X			
19. 668	X			
20. 360		X	X	
21. 4,476	X	X		
22. 1,411	X			
23. 6,000			X	
24. 14,400			X	
25. (a)	X			
26. 320	X			
27. (a)	X			
Fraudulent inventory/supply actions:				
28. 53,000	X			
29. b/766	X			
30. b/11,000	X			
31. b/64,000	X			

Description/ amount of loss	Method used by perpetrator			
	Fraudulent record initiation	Improper use of facilities	Processing alteration	Misappro- priation of output
32. (a)	X	X		
33. 3,800	X	X		
34. 13,000	X	X		
35. b/330,000	X	X		
36. 978	X			
37. 8,000	X			
38. 69,000			X	
39. (a)	X			
40. 29,000	X			
41. 12,740	X			
42. b/530,000	X			
43. 22,600	X			
44. 184	X		X	
45. 1,500	X			
46. 250,000	X			
47. 101				X
48. 1,293				X
49. 6,749				X
50. 358				X
51. 2,989				X
52. 3,074				X
53. 961				X
54. (a)				X
55. 2,609				X

Unauthorized altering
  of personnel records:

Description/ amount of loss	Fraudulent record initiation	Improper use of facilities	Processing alteration	Misappro- priation of output
56. (c)		X	X	
57. (c)		X	X	
58. (c)		X	X	
59. (c)		X	X	
60. (c)		X	X	
61. (c)		X	X	
62. (c)		X	X	
63. (c)	X	X	X	

Use of facilities
  for personal
  benefit:

Description/ amount of loss	Fraudulent record initiation	Improper use of facilities	Processing alteration	Misappro- priation of output
64. (c)		X		X
65. 1,832		X		
66. (a)		X		
67. 4,300		X		

		Method used by perpetrator			
Description/ amount of loss		Fraudulent record initiation	Improper use of facilities	Processing alteration	Misappro- priation of output
Sabotage of operations:					
68.	(a)			X	
69.	(a)	--	--	X	--
Totals	$2,161,413	d/43	d/18	d/16	d/12

Notes:

a/Loss has not been determined at the time of our review.

b/Potential loss. Crime was discovered before total loss
  occurred.

c/No monetary loss. Effect was of another type; e.g.,
  invasion of privacy.

d/Total exceeds 69 since some crimes involved more than one
  method.